Letters & Sounds

Brighter Child®
An imprint of Carson-Dellosa Publishing, LLC
P.O. Box 35665
Greensboro, NC 27425-5665

carsondellosa.com

ISBN 978-1-62057-447-8

01-060137784

Writing Tools and Safety

Using Writing Tools

Here are some tips to teach your child how to hold a pencil correctly and use it skillfully.

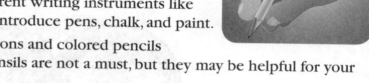

- Demonstrate how to pinch the writing utensil between your thumb and index finger and let it rest on the third finger. Encourage your child to mimic you.

- At this stage, your child may switch hand preference daily. Allow your child plenty of opportunities to experiment with using either hand. He or she will naturally establish a dominant hand.

- Let your child experiment with different writing instruments like crayons, markers, and pencils. Then, introduce pens, chalk, and paint.

- Some manufacturers make large crayons and colored pencils specifically for little hands. Large utensils are not a must, but they may be helpful for your child's first writing attempts.

Safety First

Here are some tips to make your child's first writing experiences pleasant and safe:

- Select markers, crayons, and colored pencils that are child friendly. Look for a label that says "Non Toxic and Washable."

- Remind your child that crayons, markers, pencils, and paint are for paper, not walls.

- Use a large piece of paper or a vinyl tablecloth to cover the space where you are working.

- Keep wipes or paper towels handy so you can clean marker from your child's hands.

The Letter Aa Sound

Directions: Say the sound of the letter **A**, as in *apple,* out loud to your child. Have your child say the sound with you. Ask him or her to think of an object that begins with the letter **A** sound. Have your child draw a picture of the object.

Think of a word. Draw a picture.

ACTIVITY 2

The Letter Bb Sound

Directions: Say the name of each object on the bingo card out loud to your child. Have your child draw an **X** on the objects that begin with the letter **B** sound. Encourage your child to yell "Bingo!" at the end of the activity.

Draw an **X**.

ACTIVITY 3
The Letter Cc Sound

Directions: You will need a bottle of glue for this activity. Say the names of the objects on the clouds out loud to your child. Help your child glue a cotton ball to each object that begins with the letter **C** sound. Let the glue dry completely.

Glue a cotton ball.

The Letter Dd Sound

Directions: Read the name of each doll out loud to your child. Have your child circle the dolls with names that begin with the letter **D** sound.

Circle the dolls.

Daniel

Desiree

Diego

Sophie

The Letter Ee Sound

Directions: Read the following sentence out loud to your child. Encourage your child to clap every time he or she hears the letter **E** sound. Have your child color the picture.

Ellie the elephant stands on an egg!

Color the picture.

ACTIVITY 6

The Letter Ff Sound

Directions: Farmer Fran only likes animals whose names begin with the letter **F** sound. Say the name of each animal out loud to your child. Have your child draw a line from each animal that begins with the letter **F** sound to the barn.

Draw a line.

The Letter Gg Sound

Directions: Say the sound of the letter **G**, as in *goat*, out loud to your child. Ask your child to think of a word that begins with the letter **G** sound. Encourage your child to draw the object on the grass.

Think of a word. Draw a picture.

The Letter Hh Sound

Directions: Trace your child's hand in the space below. Encourage your child to think of a word that begins with the letter **H** sound. Have your child draw the object on his or her hand.

Think of a word. Draw a picture.

The Letter Ii Sound

Directions: Say the sound of the letter **I**, as in *igloo*, out loud to your child. Have your child say the word *igloo* and point to the picture. Encourage your child to color the picture and trace the word.

Color the picture. Trace the word.

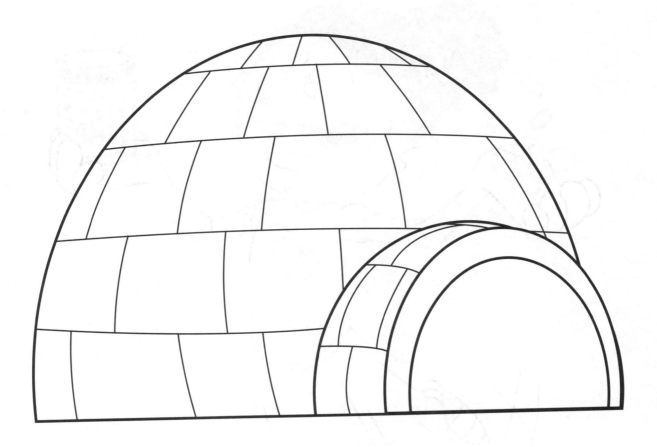

igloo

The Letter Jj Sound

Directions: Read the following sentence out loud to your child. Encourage your child to jump every time he or she hears the letter **J** sound. Have your child color the picture.

Jumping Josie jumps for jellybeans and jam.

Color the picture.

ACTIVITY 11

The Letter Kk Sound

Directions: Say the name of each object out loud to your child. Have your child point to and circle each object that begins with the letter **K** sound.

Point to the pictures. Circle the pictures.

The Letter Ll Sound

Directions: Say the name of each object out loud to your child. Have your child point to the objects that begin with the letter **L** sound. Encourage your child to draw a line from each object that begins with the letter **L** sound to the lemon lollipop.

Draw a line.

The Letter Mm Sound

Directions: Say the sound of the letter **M**, as in *milk*, out loud to your child. Have your child say the sound with you. Ask your child to think of an object that begins with the letter **M** sound. Have your child draw a picture of the object on the milk carton.

Think of a word. Draw a picture.

GRADE A • PASTEURIZED • HOMOGENIZED

The Letter Nn Sound

Directions: Say the name of each object out loud to your child. Have your child draw an **X** on the objects that begin with the letter **N** sound.

Draw an **X**.

The Letter Oo Sound

Directions: You will need a bottle of glue for this activity. Say the name of each object out loud to your child. Help your child glue a piece of **o**-shaped cereal to each object that begins with the letter **O** sound. Let the glue dry completely.

Glue a piece of cereal.

ACTIVITY 16
The Letter Pp Sound

Directions: You will need a bottle of glue for this activity. Say the name of each object out loud to your child. Help your child glue a penny to each object that begins with the letter **P** sound. Let the glue dry completely. (Safety Tip: Never leave your child alone with small objects.)

Glue a penny.

The Letter Qq Sound

Directions: Read the following sentence out loud to your child. Encourage your child to stomp every time he or she hears the letter **Q** sound. Have your child color the picture.

Quinn the Queen quits quilting whenever it's quiet.

Color the picture.

The Letter Rr Sound

Directions: Ralph the Rabbit loves to race! Help your child get Ralph to the finish line. Say the name of each object out loud to your child. Have your child draw a line through the maze by connecting each word that begins with the letter **R** sound.

Draw a line.

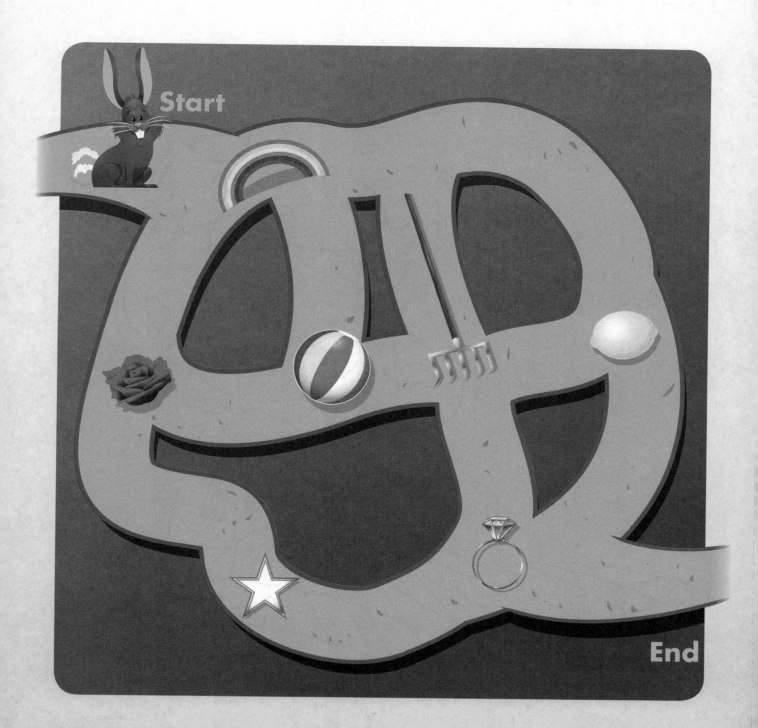

The Letter Ss Sound

Directions: Say the sound of the letter **S**, as in *sun*, out loud to your child. Ask your child to think of a word that begins with the letter **S** sound. Encourage your child to draw the object beneath the sun.

Think of a word. Draw a picture.

The Letter Tt Sound

Directions: Trace your child's foot in the space below and count his or her toes. Encourage your child to think of a word that begins with the letter **T** sound. Have your child draw a picture of the object on his or her foot.

Think of a word. Draw a picture.

The Letter Uu Sound

Directions: Say the sound of the letter **U**, as in *unhappy*, out loud to your child. Have your child say the word *unhappy* and point to the picture. Encourage your child to color the picture and trace the word.

Color the picture. Trace the word.

unhappy

The Letter Vv Sound

Directions: Read the following sentence out loud to your child. Encourage your child to clap every time he or she hears the letter **V** sound. Have your child color the picture.

The violin was in the violet van.

Color the picture.

The Letter Ww Sound

Directions: Say the name of each object out loud to your child. Have your child point to and circle each object that begins with the letter **W** sound.

Point to the pictures. Circle the pictures.

The Letter Xx Sound

Directions: Say the name of each object out loud to your child. Have your child point to the objects that contain the letter **X** sound at the end of the word. Encourage your child to draw a line from each object that contains the letter **X** sound to the fox in the box.

Draw a line.

The Letter Yy Sound

Directions: Say the sound of the letter **Y**, as in *yellow*, out loud to your child. Have your child say the sound with you. Ask your child to think of an object that begins with the letter **Y** sound. Have your child draw a picture of the object.

Think of a word. Draw a picture.

The Letter Zz Sound

Directions: Say the sound of the letter **Z**, as in *zebra*, out loud to your child. Have your child say the word *zebra* and point to the picture. Encourage your child to draw black stripes on the zebra and trace the word.

Draw stripes. Trace the word.

zebra

Alphabet Match

Directions: Point to each letter and say its name. Encourage your child to draw a line from each letter to the object that begins with that letter's sound.

Draw a line.

B

C

F

G

J

L

O

R

T

Y

ACTIVITY 28

Alphabet Match

Directions: Point to each letter and say its name. Encourage your child to draw a line from each letter to the object that begins with that letter's sound.

Draw a line.

A   D   E   I   K   N   Q   S   V   Z

Missing Letters

Directions: Help your child fill in the missing letters of the alphabet. Start at the letter **A**. Read each letter out loud to your child. When you come to a missing letter, pause and let your child identify which letter comes next. Ask him or her to write the missing letter on the line.

Write the missing letter.

A B _____ **D**

E F _____ **H I**

_____ **K L M**

_____ **O P** _____

Missing Letters

Directions: Continue to help your child fill in the missing letters of the alphabet. Read each letter out loud to your child. When you come to a missing letter, pause and let your child identify which letter comes next. Ask him or her to write the missing letter on the line.

Write the missing letter.

R S T ___ V

W ___ Y Z